HURLING WORDS INTO DARKNESS

A Book Doctor's Dose of Brain Science for Writers

Also by Peter Gelfan

Monkey Temple
Found Objects

Hurling Words into Darkness

A Book Doctor's Dose of Brain Science for Writers

By

PETER GELFAN

Adelaide Books
New York / Lisbon
2021

HURLING WORDS INTO DARKNESS
By Peter Gelfan

Copyright © by Peter Gelfan
Cover design © 2021 Adelaide Books

Published by Adelaide Books, New York / Lisbon
adelaidebooks.org

Editor-in-Chief
Stevan V. Nikolic

For any information, please address Adelaide Books
at info@adelaidebooks.org

or write to:

Adelaide Books
244 Fifth Ave. Suite D27
New York, NY, 10001

ISBN: 978-1-955196-67-3

Printed in the United States of America

Contents

cont'd...

I would hurl words into this darkness and wait for an echo, and if an echo sounded, no matter how faintly, I would send other words to tell, to march, to fight, to create a sense of hunger for life that gnaws in us all, to keep alive in our hearts a sense of the inexpressibly human.

—Richard Wright, writer

Why Another Book on Writing?

Some years ago, during a bout of singleness, I walked into a small Vermont inn and found a party going on, an engagement celebration for a couple I'd never met. But I knew a few of the guests, and there was plenty of food, an open bar, and lively company, so what the hell. When I went for my first glass, a pretty blond sat alone at the bar. We started talking.

"What do you do?" she asked.

"I'm a writer."

She shrugged. "Anybody can write."

I could have argued, but that wasn't why I'd struck up a conversation with her. I asked what she did.

She sat up a little straighter and shook her hair back from her face. "I'm a singer."

I couldn't keep a snarky grin from snaking across my face. "Everybody sings."

She laughed. "Okay, I see what you mean."

And we've been together ever since? No, the conversation petered out after a few minutes, and I never saw her again. So much for frank exchanges during courtship.

But the question remains: what distinguishes a successful writer from one of the million others who write?

The dirty little not-so secret of the publishing industry is that except for having an already bestselling or celebrity author, there is no reliable way of predicting how well a book will do if published. Most veteran agents and acquisitions editors have stories of a manuscript they loved but which never found an audience, and of others they deemed a nonstarter but, in the hands of another agent or publisher, became a success. Likewise, thousands of writers have followed to the letter a book or course that purported to tell them how to write a blockbuster, only to watch their manuscript stack up rejections while other books, some of them breaking those same hard-learned rules, became hits. A few agents and editors are known for having The Eye, for being able to spot a winner in a crowd. Maybe so. But let's not forget that the mere fact of being plucked from the clamoring throng by such an august figure makes a manuscript and its author buzzworthy.

Because so many unpredictable elements are involved— luck, timing, real or imagined market trends, the personal tastes and moods of individual gatekeepers, an evolving concept of fiction and nonfiction, and the random nature of existence—no one can honestly tell writers how to get published.

However, while writers have no surefire path to success, there are some reliably watertight guarantors of failure. It's interesting that the lethal mistakes, whether in fiction or nonfiction, are relatively few and overwhelmingly common. (Agents and acquisitions editors surely yearn for fresh, fascinating, even enlightening reasons to say no to a manuscript.) As Ernest Hemingway said, "We are all apprentices in a craft where no one ever becomes a master." He was talking about writers but could just as well have included editors, agents, and publishers.

I once heard an art teacher say that a budding painter can learn far more from looking at second-rate art than from studying the masters. You stand in awe of a transcendent canvas, but its creator, like a magician, doesn't show you much about how she did it. On the other hand, an unsuccessful painting's problems and mistakes are on lurid display. As a freelance book editor, I have read a frightening number of manuscripts, some by established or bestselling authors who needed help with a particular section or problem, but most by writers who had not yet been able to find a publisher or even an agent. Agents, publishers, and movie producers enjoy the efficient luxury of having to read a ms only as far as it takes to find a reason to say no. But if you're paid to read the whole thing, you do so, carefully, and try your best to figure out and explain to the author what is and isn't working and why. And then you often discuss it in detail with the writer and discover what led him astray.

The terminal surface flaws have been listed many times— lackluster characters, slack or predictable plot, unconvincing dialogue, copycatting, amateurish or insipid writing, flat voice, etc.—and a number of how-to books already exist on remedying these problems. A book editor must look beyond the faults on the page and try to understand what went wrong with the writer's thinking. Again and again, it turns out that likewise, the writer had better look beyond his own agenda and try to understand what's going on in readers' minds.

In the mid-twentieth century, writer and scientist C. P. Snow warned that human culture was threatened by a growing schism between the arts and science. He noted that his friends in the arts were ignorant about science, while most scientists he knew tended to ignore the arts. Yet how can any of us claim to be educated or cultured without interest and knowledge in both? He called this problem "the two cultures," and it's more prevalent now than it was then.

For thousands of years we've had theories and rules about writing based on tradition, philosophy, esthetics, poetics, scholarship, mysticism, and arbitrary dictates. Meanwhile, over only the past few decades, cognitive science has discovered much about how the human mind sees and orders the world and extracts meaning from it. It's high time we mix some brain science into our thinking about reading and writing. That's what this treatise attempts to do.

Hurling Words into Darkness is not step-by-step how-to. Plenty of other books provide specific advice. This one, by introducing some basic neuroscientific concepts, hopes to give writers x-ray glasses for their own work, help them think for themselves in new ways, and guide them around the Sirens of screwing it all up. Some of the material relates specifically to fiction, but much is also applicable to nonfiction. Many of the same principles apply, and plenty of good nonfiction—especially history, biography, and narrative nonfiction, which includes memoir—borrows copiously from fiction technique.

I have read a lot of books about writing, writers, reading, and readers and will do my best not to repeat things you may have read elsewhere. This piece is a summary of what I have learned over decades of editing manuscripts and studying scientific research into the human mind and brain, but have rarely found in books about writing.

I won't tell you how to write your novel or script. Your creativity, imagination, originality, skill, and hard work are what will make your manuscripts wonderful. I can only help you avoid some of the fatal errors and suggest a deeper perspective on what we're doing, how, and why.

Why Write? Why Read?

Why does a writer write? Writers, writing teachers, writing students, writers' conferences, and writing groups seem to endlessly discuss this question. Sure, it's an interesting topic, but after a while, a suspicion insinuates itself into the heady atmosphere. One imagines a smoky bar, four tortured figures hunched over their cheap bourbons around a wobbly table, a country song whining softly from a gap-toothed jukebox.

"Why do we spend our days doing what we do?"

"I never thought I'd end up like this."

"This game just isn't what it's cracked up to be."

"Where's the glamour, the money, the beautiful lonely housewives?"

"It's all hard work, sore backs, grime and stink everywhere."

"So why do we plumbers plumb?"

Might writers discuss why we write simply because, like everybody else, we like to talk about ourselves?

We all have our own reasons for writing, some conscious, some not. Our individual motives and desires don't necessarily have any bearing on a more urgent question most of us have: how can I get lots of people to buy and read my damn book?

Too many first drafts, not only of nonfiction, begin with a preface or introduction explaining why the author wrote the book. A more pertinent question to address in an intro, preface, or flap copy, whether directly or by implication, is why the person holding the book should read it. And a far more answerable and productive general question for any writer is why do readers read?

In a happy if often lucky confluence of motives, sometimes a writer writes what he or she wants to, and it just so happens to mesh with what many readers want to read and perhaps catches a zeitgeist before anyone—usually including the writer—notices the trend. Later, once a market is established, plenty of writers work to tap into it, whether it's for terrorism thrillers, gritty memoir, true crime, or explicitly sexual romance novels. Wherever a writer is on that continuum, from devil-may-caringly doing one's own thing to slavishly catering to a bustling and probably overstocked niche market, putting some thought and research into why readers read can be useful and enlightening.

Every human culture tells stories. Some are meant to chronicle supposedly actual events, whether it's a creation story or the history of a family, city, or country. Others are explicitly fictional, such as fables, tall tales, and fairytales. It's interesting that fiction can be just as effective as nonfiction, or even more so, in eliciting emotional response. Why did one made-up story about a killer shark off New England (*Jaws*) change the emotional outlook and behavior of far more people than did thousands of news items about smokers who died of lung cancer?

Anthropologists often try to determine whether a specific human trait has its roots in our shared biology or in an individual's culture. The answer often lies in a simple question: do only some cultures have this trait or do all humans have it? Language is an interesting example. We have many human languages, each of us learns the one that our parents and neighbors speak, and so our specific language is clearly a cultural trait. But at the same time, all humans everywhere avidly learn the language into which they are born, and so the use of language itself is a biological, genetic trait.

The universality of storytelling among human cultures strongly suggests it's not simply a cultural trait but is also inborn. It's literally in our DNA. Stories run like blood through our neural pathways. Storytelling and story-listening are an innate part of being human—we're born with it.

But why?

"Nothing in biology makes sense except in the light of evolution." ~ Theodosius Dobzhansky, geneticist.

Just about any creature can and must learn from its own experiences. A few can learn by witnessing the experiences of others of their kind. Humans can also learn from hearing about other people's experiences without having been there to see the events and thereby also to face the same dangers. We have turned this talent into prolific art—literally—and it's a prime basis of our culture.

The capacity to acquire survival knowledge risk-free might well be the Darwinian hook in our enjoyment of reading in whatever form. We all safely learn survival skills from hearing about the dangers, predicaments, or heartbreak others have seen or been through. And we all, by telling our stories and passing along others', raise not only our own chances of survival but also those of our children, families, friends, tribe, and, as the stories travel elsewhere, of the whole human race.

Okay, that makes sense, except that most of us don't read for life lessons, we read for pleasure.

We also eat not because of a rational understanding of the need for nutrition but because we're hungry and food tastes good. We usually have sex not to produce children but because it feels so good—in fact, we often go out of our way to make sure it doesn't produce children. Our nervous systems have evolved to use pleasure to lure us into doing things that will lead to staying alive and reproducing, as well as using pain and fear to bully us into avoiding danger. Likewise, people read fiction primarily to be entertained in the broadest sense of the word—to have a good time, to be inspired by a soaring story, to get away from their own humdrum or torturous lives, to be transported, to cry and laugh and scream and fear for their lives in the safety and comfort of their own airplane seats, and to take a peek at other lives, settings, and eras. Along the way, they will learn something from it. We read war stories, for example, to experience war without having to experience war. The lessons of vicarious experience may not bite as deeply as those learned first-hand, but they're fun, time-economical—we can absorb years of experience in a couple of hours—and much less likely to be fatal.

Of course we're not all out every day wrestling mastodons or fighting wars. Most of our challenges are societal—dealing with other people at school, at work, in business, at home, in romance, in childrearing, in travels. Likewise, most stories these days depict modern problems and conflicts and provide a wide range of experience for us to digest. Survival isn't about just life and death, but also about quality of life for us and our families.

We all crave and fear experience. Reading is a safe, easy way to bulk up on it. While we experience stories as entertainment, they function as prepackaged units of defanged thirdhand experience—a sort of vaccination in case the real thing arrives. They help us as individuals and cultures to cope, learn, grow, survive, and thrive.

Puppies and kittens play at stalking and fighting; children play soldier and house. Like these activities, reading isn't only a pleasurable pastime but also a vital survival pursuit. As we read, listen to, or watch a story, we inject ourselves into the narrative, assess the situation, offer (or shout) advice to the hero, or imagine what we would do in such a situation. It feels like play but helps us stay alive. According to neuroscientist Daniel J. Levitan, "…when we see someone else get hurt, even from a scene in a movie, we wince as if we, too, are being harmed. The evolutionary basis for this may be to help us learn about aversive things without having to go through them ourselves."

The three levels of experience: firsthand, it happens to you; secondhand, you see it happen to another; thirdhand, you hear about it happening to someone else. You learn the most from firsthand, less from secondhand, and even less from third-hand. But a gripping, well-told story pushes the transmitted thirdhand experience up as close as possible to firsthand in two stages. First, vivid storytelling boosts the account from third-hand toward secondhand—you do see it happen, even if in your imagination. Then, empathy with the characters moves it up toward firsthand—you see it as though it's happening to you. Stories are life training without life consequences.

This process is not just a matter of our brains becoming attuned to stories. It cuts much deeper than that. I doubt there was any such thing as stories before humans invented them. Our minds have evolved to make sense of the world in terms of cause-effect chains of events that we have come to call stories. These packets of condensed understanding may be simplistic and somewhat inaccurate, but they serve us well as rough charts by which to navigate life, especially when we don't have time for deeper thought before having to make a decision. As Daniel Kahneman, Nobel Prize winner and author of *Thinking, Fast and Slow* puts it, "This is how the remembering self works: it composes stories and keeps them for future reference."

Anthropologists tell us that the development of spoken language and then writing enabled individual humans to amass more knowledge than was possible for earlier, prelinguistic and preliterate people. We can also say that written stories allow us to amass more experience, and more-varied experience, than preliterate people can.

The literary spectrum stretches from straight nonfiction through narrative nonfiction to fiction. One end consists of pure lessons or knowledge without touching on the experiences of acquiring them—technology, textbooks, and so on. At the other end of the spectrum lies pure experience without any explicit statement of lesson or meaning—art, including many forms of storytelling. The fiction/nonfiction dichotomy is somewhat illusory. Nonfiction can be inadvertently or deliberately false, while fiction can be close to fact; nonfiction sometimes tells a riveting story, while some fiction can be virtually plotless. The more important distinction is how much emotional and intellectual credence the reader grants the narrative—how subjectively "true" it seems to be. The experiential process goes beyond the so-called willing suspension of disbelief: not only could this happen, but it could happen to me, and I'd better be ready for it.

At the lesson end of the spectrum, explicit information is transferred to the reader, presumably for some useful purpose—Italian vocabulary, a pie recipe, how to poison your husband and leave no trace using only the cosmetics on your dressing table. At the experience end, there is no Aesop's-fable moral. Instead, the book (or movie or play) puts readers through an ersatz experience that stimulates many of their cognitive faculties—emotions, intellect, imagination, senses, sexuality, intuition, humor, morality—and actively involves readers in the story's situations, feelings, and ideas, from which they can't help but learn things at various levels.

We may ask ourselves, or a teacher may ask us, what was the author trying to convey? We can never really know that, and the author may not know even if he tells anecdotes about why he wrote it. What matters is what the individual reader takes away from the story, for that meaning will be far more relevant and useful to him or her.

This defines the task and art of storytelling and differentiates it from expository nonfiction. The novelist, scriptwriter, or monologist isn't primarily informing, educating, or lecturing readers. He or she is creating a venue for experience. A story is effective to the degree that it immerses the reader into its world, characters, and events. Each reader will perceive the experience, react to it, interpret it, and perhaps in some manner change because of it, all in ways different from other readers. "A story teaches us to make new mistakes rather than recursively repeating the old." ~ Coco Krumme, mathematician.

Your Message

The approach to storytelling I just described makes many first-time novelists nervous. They may have a theme, a message, a dialectical premise to expound and prove, or an outlook on life to promote, and they want to make sure their readers understand it exactly as intended. Often a character will "realize" the message or interpret the story's meaning in extended interior monologue and/or explain it in dialogue. But these novels often come across as pedantic, didactic, and self-serving, and so rarely make it past the publication gatekeepers or into readers' hearts.

Unless you're a famous novelist with something of a cult following, readers aren't the least bit interested in your philosophy of life no matter how profound and fascinating you may find it. If they want explicit life lessons, they'll hunt the philosophy, self-help, or inspirational shelves, not fiction. On the other hand, readers will accept an engrossing, thought-provoking, mind-expanding story from anyone who can tell it well.

With most good storytelling, the author isn't so much trying to get readers to understand *his* opinions, ideas, and assumptions as to examine, perhaps for the first time, their own. He does this by putting characters, with whom readers can empathize, through an ordeal. The most effective messages don't come one-size-fits-all straight from the author, but from readers themselves, as a consequence of their own very individual emotional involvement with and reaction to the characters and their ordeal. The astute writer guides readers by choosing the characters, the ordeal, and the outcome, but entrusts interpretation to readers. As Hannah Arendt puts it, "Storytelling reveals meaning without committing the error of defining it." Failure to understand and act upon this principle is one of the hallmarks of unagented, unpublished, unread novels.

Instead, novelists can embrace the idea that they haven't created only one experience, one journey, one meaning, but rather a vehicle and a roadmap for thousands of readers on their own journeys. This indeterminacy is why I call a novel a venue for experience rather than the experience itself. The actual experience isn't on the page. The story only stimulates reader imagination to create the experience.

Neophyte screenwriters are often told that a screenplay isn't a work of art but a blueprint for one, awaiting the creative contributions of the director, actors, cinematographer, composer, set and costume designers, and so on. Similarly, a novel is a blueprint for the sort of experience you want readers' imaginations to bring to life. If a screenplay goes into too much detail about the setting, the characters' every move, emotion, and facial expression and the angle of every shot, then the director, actors, and cinematographer (if things ever get that far) will resent the micromanagement for hobbling their creativity. Likewise, a novel or memoir that tries to spell out and explain everything in explicit detail—characters' backgrounds, motives, emotions, thoughts, meanings, moral judgments—will tend to stifle reader imagination and participation and thus undermine its power to conjure up an experience.

Readers are supposed to empathize with the characters; it helps if the writer can empathize with readers. You have to piggyback your desires on theirs. Give them what they want—at least long enough to bring about engagement with your story or material and some trust in you—and then, as long as you maintain that bond, you can take things wherever you like.

Subtext

In any story, especially a subtle one, much of what's most important is never put into words. Just as dialogue has subtext—unspoken meanings, nuances, implications—so do actions and everything else in a novel, play, or movie. It's what gives any writing depth. Putting into words what would better be left implied yanks it to the surface, thus losing depth and depriving readers of the pleasures of peering into those depths and trying to discern what swims there. This process is what turns the tale into an experience for them. To accomplish this, a writer must be willing and even eager for the story to be distinctly the reader's experience rather than a copy of his own.

Profundity doesn't come so much from what you say as from what you stimulate readers to speculate about, and that often requires refraining from saying things, which can be torture for a writer. Reader speculation is often framed in terms of wondering what the author means. The wise author usually declines to explain herself. The writer hands readers the story. Readers then search for explanations—and to find them, they have to put themselves in the characters' shoes and search their own souls. That's how stories affect and change people. If the writer provides the explanations, the story loses its depth and power. If Leonardo had attached a little sign to the *Mona Lisa* saying who she is and why she's smiling, do you think the painting would still be so famous, loved, valuable, and talked about?

Paradoxically, the storyteller's essential art is to communicate through human interaction rather than by verbal explanation. You may be concerned that readers exactly understand your ideas, feelings, and meanings, but it's more important, and better literature, to get them to look at, or arrive at, their own. Write for smart readers, and your writing will be smarter.

Angels and Devils

People have always used stories for other ends than just to entertain and implicitly teach survival skills. A story well put together has a ring of truth about it. Our brains will lap it up and store it away for further use. People make up and/or relay stories for all sorts of reasons, usually with some degree of self-interest and sometimes to the detriment of listeners, readers, or watchers. I can't think of a religion that doesn't have an origin story, some of them quite beautiful and scary. Every country has its heroic national myth. Advertisers use stories to sell. Unverified rumors, gossip, and conspiracy theories can be too juicy not to pass on. An effective story makes us want it to be true, and then deciding it is true gives us a burst of pleasure, especially if it seems to explain something. It's rather addicting. For better or for worse, stories can nudge us in directions we would never have come up with on our own.

One antidote might consist of judging every supposedly true story we hear as to how likely it is to be factual, but that could take up a lot of time. Can we at least refrain from passing on such stories until we establish plausibility, necessity, and the right thing to do? Meanwhile, some schools now do try to teach their students critical thinking. And yet the curriculum still demands that kids parrot back a glorified, sanitized, national myth.

Rules vs. Creativity

Storytelling has of course developed far beyond cave-fire, kill-or-be-killed narratives. It has become art, culture, excursions into new ways of seeing and thinking. But its visceral, prehistoric hook is still what keeps us avid for stories and what makes those stories compelling. To take full advantage of this cognitive mechanism humankind has evolved, a writer might aim not to act on readers as passive spectators, as if lecturing an audience, but to engage them as active co-creators, as if guiding them through an adventure.

Looking at storytelling as a way to provide readers with experience for their enjoyment and erudition (even if subliminal) doesn't beget a whole new set of so-called rules for writing. The entire point is to gain a deeper understanding of the process so that you, as an artist, can accomplish it in your own way.

"…an evolutionary account of art, far from being reductive or deterministic, can do more than any other to explain art's force and freedom." ~ Brian Boyd, *On the Origin of Stories*

The rest of this treatise expands upon writing habits that may work for or against this goal, outlines more of the brain science behind it, and suggests ways to achieve it.

Characters

In his book *The Storytelling Animal*, Jonathan Gottschall boils down story to a simple equation: Story = Character + Predicament + Attempted extrication. Humans have apparently always been social creatures, and while we have had to contend with the forces of nature, sometimes personified as spirits or gods, most human predicaments and attempted extrications have consisted of other people—characters. This has become truer as we have grown increasingly clustered and cooperativized. Over the millennia, for more and more people, the landscape and its creatures have become less of an immediate threat, and it's mostly people we have to contend with. One can imagine a story without a plot, without dialogue, without almost anything except a character. So let's start here.

The principle of vicarious experience applies especially to the treatment of characters, for that experience comes about by readers' temporarily living inside characters' skins and walking in their shoes. Some of the most common and debilitating errors made by first-time novelists concern characters.

"We sometimes encounter people, even perfect strangers, who begin to interest us at first sight, somehow suddenly, all at once, before a word has been spoken." ~ Dostoyevsky, *Crime and Punishment*

In real life, nothing revs up our cognitive faculties as much as does encountering an interesting person. We look them over, listen to their sounds, discreetly sniff them, and often touch them with a handshake—firm and warm, or clammy, limp, skittish, caressive, aggressively gripping, or clingy. We listen to them talk, not so much to reap explicit information as to get a feel for them. What do they choose to talk about: politics, quantum physics, celebrity scandal, or, God forbid, themselves? What's the tone—confident, snide, conspiratorial, haughty, affectionate, nervous, argumentative? Does this person have something I want? Might he or she want something I have? Are we potential friends, rivals, enemies, lovers, colleagues? How does she regard me—oh, my God, hasn't she even noticed me? Within the first half minute of meeting someone who strikes us as worthy of notice, our feverish imaginations put us through several lifetimes with them. The same thing should happen to readers upon first introduction to a major character in a novel, play, or movie.

Theory of Mind

In philosophy, zoology, and cognitive science, the term *theory of mind* (or sometimes *intentional stance*) refers to the ability of humans and some other species to speculate about what another person or creature is thinking, feeling, or planning based on its appearance, conduct, and mien. We cannot know for sure what is going on in the other's mind, but we have the capacity to form a theory, a best guess, based on present observation and earlier experience, about what it might be. The predictive speculation helps us prepare an optimum response. Two bull moose face off. Perhaps the older, bigger, but weakening one detects a muted flinch in the upstart and calculates that a fast, preemptive charge will rout the younger one without a protracted battle. A bird pretends to have a broken wing to lure the cat away from the nest, and as it fake-hobbles, it keeps an eye on the cat to make sure the ruse is working. As to how reasoned and conscious these behaviors are, that's a different question. Clearly the animals (and people) are watching one another and in some manner calculating responses based on what they see, hear, smell, and remember. With humans, it can get quite layered. I know that my new boss knows that I know that she knows that I was a friend of her predecessor, and I also know that she knows that I have the CEO's ear, but does she know I argued with him against hiring her? I watch for clues. This is the stuff of human life.

"Theory of mind is why humans write novels and why they read them." So says Rebecca Saxe, neuroscientist, in the Dec. 2012 issue of *Scientific American*. She has located the precise part of the mammalian brain where much of this function takes place. That structure is highly developed in humans.

The 18 Oct. 2013 issue of *Science* published "Reading Literary Fiction Improves Theory of Mind," an article chronicling the results of a study conducted at the New School in New York City showing that reading novels that focus on characters' inner lives and relationships improved readers' abilities to understand what others are thinking and feeling and even to imagine their motives and interior monologue. This is essentially what is meant by empathy (as opposed to sympathy): to some degree, readers become that character, experience her ordeal, and learn something from it.

Theory of mind is one of the core life skills we hone through hearing, reading, or watching stories. On the surface, we experience it as entertainment in the form of mystery, suspense, and character speculation, but the key phenomenon is empathy—imagining ourselves as that character. We rarely also think of it as a mental workout to tone our brains for the following day on the job or the next social event.

Creating Characters

When creating a new character for a novel, a writer often approaches the task in a utilitarian way, just as we might hire someone. If we need a toilet fixed, we hire a licensed plumber. A character needs a boyfriend, so we write a guy about her age, decent looking but no movie star, employed but not rich, likes wine but no drunk, done. And now the plot has the necessary plausible boyfriend.

But have we missed something?

Characters need to be diligent in more than just their story duties. In fiction, every character has two separate functions: to play the role called for in the story and, aside from plot, to act as a channel of engagement between readers and the story's world. A character shouldn't be a mere functionary but should also, as a distinct person, draw readers in—like that stranger you meet at a party. Rather than just a sidekick, he can be a Falstaff or a Sancho Panza, an asset in his own right. Instead of the obligatory wife, she can be a Carmela Soprano, who by her manner and way of speaking makes readers relish the prospect of seeing more of her and wonder what she really thinks about her husband and his line of work.

This doesn't mean characters need to be cute, quirky, or grotesque. In essence, readers have to see them as interesting, original, even unique, have an emotional reaction to them, and begin to ascribe hidden depths to them.

To do this, we must go beyond the character's curriculum vitae. Sure, some specific, plot-related elements may be needed in their personalities (perhaps distrust) or backstory (maybe a public disgrace). Those are the requisite facts. From there, instead of coming up with a few more off-the-shelf traits or backstory, let imagination take over. Who is this individual?

At the heart of this creation is the character's motivation. Much has been said about this, including layers of motivation: conscious and stated motivation, conscious but unstated (secret) motives, unconscious urges perhaps eventually revealed to self and/or others over the course of the story. Motivation can be complex. Half the time (optimistically low estimate) we don't even know why we do what we do. Often in literature, as in life, instead of conscious motivation sparking action, action reveals hidden motivation. For readers, the learning experience amounts to a theory-of-mind workout. For the writer, this approach often requires an overhaul of characterization technique.

Cognitive science in the previous few decades has established as fact what many writers have suspected for millennia: human beings are masters of self-deception. Robert Trivers goes into this in depth in his book *The Folly of Fools*. If human intelligence, which we love to lord over other species, is our defining quality, then why do we, as individuals and cultures, practice self-deceit on a grand and pervasive scale? We lie to ourselves about ourselves, how others view us, our pasts, what we see or don't see, what we know and don't know, and our certainty about all these things.

If we're so damn smart, how has self-deceit survived the rigors of natural selection? Trivers's answer begins with straightforward logic. All animals practice deceit—to catch prey, evade predators, one-up competitors, and attract mates. To a large degree, evolution is an arms race between competing individuals and species in deception technique and detection. The gotcha in all this is that our efforts to deceive others are usually more convincing and harder for others to see through if we believe our own lies, and so self-deception became built into our hardware.

Deception is the basis of our literary art: we make up believable stories. That same literary art can also be sabotaged by one of self-deception's most common symptoms, over-confidence. We finish a first draft convinced we have a work of genius in hand that better get to market right away before someone steals it or we get hit by a truck. Skip revisions, to hell with self-editing, forget about letting it lie fallow for a week or two and coming back to it, and who needs test readers?

At times, overconfidence has great value. In life-or-death situations, we have a few seconds or at best minutes to come up with a solution, and our minds quickly scan the possibilities—attack, flee, deceive, negotiate? And we settle upon what seems to be the most favorable or least dubious solution. But then, when it comes time to put that solution into action, it's more likely to work if we do so wholeheartedly, fully confident, with no doubts snagging our attention or slowing us down. Hence the outbreak of overconfidence, an instant supercharger for our actions.

That all makes sense for the sort of dire situations our prehistoric ancestors were likely to face. Meanwhile, we live in different times with more or less the same brain. We often make choices when that brain pushes us into overconfident emergency mode when in fact we have plenty of time to be thorough and think things through. The certainty of overconfidence feels so much better than the anxiety of uncertainty. For writers, despite authorial self-deception, as Hemingway noted, "The first draft of anything is shit."

Even the concept of the self has been thrown into doubt. We like to think of ourselves, and often a fictional character, as a rational, keen-eyed, clear-headed captain who pilots the ship of self through the sea of life. It sounds good and has been the accepted paradigm of human existence since before the pyramids were built. It has also been a fundamental assumption of many social sciences and of our own self-image. Why let a few sordid facts spoil such a beautiful theory?

Yet the closer science drills down to finding this self, the more elusive it becomes. Our self as Mom or Dad is very different from our self at work, or behind the wheel, or on vacation, or visiting the in-laws. We seem to be a collection of varying, wavering selves. The brain deftly plasters over the cracks to give the comforting illusion of oneness, of singular I-ness, but could the whole idea of a self be a useful illusion—or, as we say in the biz, a convincing fiction? I'll leave it to you to decide whether self-deception is still a useful brain feature or now a vestigial bug.

In any case, creating a character isn't like designing a machine part that will reliably do the same thing over and over in a deterministic way. It's not a matter of just coming up with a physical description, listing a couple of distinct traits, sketching a backstory, and then strictly adhering to those specs for the next 400 pages. Of course you need some guidelines, but what you want to begin with is a character who can work with and grow with your story. You can fill in the details as you go along—and then again later as you revise.

Your characters are also subject to self-deception. They can plan to do something then chicken out or fail to follow up. They can rationalize their own actions, misunderstand or misconstrue situations and other people, or misremember. The so-called *unreliable narrator* relates or interprets a story's events differently than readers do, which, as well as creating an interesting counterpoint, helps suggest who this character might be. The idea isn't to sharply define the character—leave that for readers to fill in for themselves as they move through the story—but to suggest what he or she might or might not be capable of, which readers' theory-of-mind faculties can then chew over.

Sometimes a character will climb up out of the creative depths more or less fully formed or will quickly take on a distinct personality as soon as you begin to write him or her. If not, here's one way to breathe life into the mannequin. Picture this person in your mind. Give her a job interview, so to speak, perhaps by having her encounter your main character in a work or social situation. They strike up a conversation—you can write it, or just watch it unfold in your imagination. Instead of playing puppet master and feeding her lines, wait and see what she does. If at first she just sits there waiting for you to issue orders, outwait her. It's almost meditative. Simply watch her without making suggestions. Sooner or later, she'll do something, or at least you'll notice something about her reticence. Or your main character will act, and you can watch the new character's responses. Observe her smile or frown, listen to her tone of voice. Can she make you or your main character laugh? Can she surprise you? Does your main character have a strong reaction to her? If she's too bland, give her a barbed wit or an adventurous approach to life and see what she does with it. If too obnoxious, endow her with, say, a knack for amusing other people's children. Keep working with her until she can elicit emotion from your main character and thoroughly delight you.

That's what you want for all your characters: to have minds of their own and to surprise and even defy you as you continue to write them. As writer Milan Kundera observed, an artist's work is more intelligent than the artist. Part of that synergy for a novelist, I believe, lies in listening to your characters, who may sometimes have a better idea than you do for a line of dialogue, a scene, or a plot development. Does taking advice from your characters mean you're slightly crazy? As a writer, surely you already knew that. But another way to look at it is that the traits, actions, dialogue, feelings, and thoughts of your characters that you didn't premeditate for them probably originate in the hidden parts of your mind and can even give you a glimpse into your own inner workings—and, you hope, do the same for readers.

If your characters start challenging you and mutinying, that's a good sign that you have brought them to life. You can create characters to be whatever you want, but once you do, in order for them to be convincing, you have to give them their head rather than force them to obey you. From a practical point of view, this often means unobtrusively manipulating other elements so that things still go in the same general direction you planned, but perhaps by a different route.

And if you later decide, for the sake of the story, that you have to change the character's initial personality, then you'd better also go back to the beginning and revamp everything that character does or says to bring it in line with your changes, which may in turn affect other characters and events.

It almost goes without saying that the story's ordeal should be dire enough to bring about development—create changes—in the major characters, unless your point is that one of them cannot change. It also stands to reason that character development in stories might subliminally make readers more receptive to change in themselves.

In the end, this all comes down to creativity. With a new character, you don't want simply the right sort of cog to fit into your narrative machine, an efficient player who has the qualifications to do the job. Give readers more than they anticipate, a character who overturns their expectations and, getting back to our caveperson origins, who matters to them and so whose experiences will pack a punch and make them (and perhaps you) look at the world in a different way.

Introducing Characters

Characters, especially the protagonist, must engage readers: specifically, they have to make us want to spend a novel with them. We can love them, hate them, fear them or fear for them, but they have to inspire strong enough emotions to bind us to them.

"Call me Ishmael," *Moby-Dick* famously opens. What an odd way to introduce oneself—an abrupt command and a hint that the narrator may be hiding his real name or harboring biblical delusions of grandeur. He then launches into a short, pithy rant to the effect that when burnt out from dealing with morons and clowns ashore, he goes to sea to chill. Most readers feel compelled to keep reading simply because Ishmael as a character promises a good story with a lively narrator.

Two other first-page major-character intros:

> He—for there could be no doubt of his sex, though the fashion of the time did something to disguise it—was in the act of slicing at the head of a Moor which swung from the rafters. (*Orlando*, Virginia Woolf)

> "This is the worst day of my life," you say, as you drop a salted peanut into your double martini—on better days, you drink white wine—and watch it sink. (*Half Asleep in Frog Pajamas*, Tom Robbins)

The dynamics of these three openings are instructive, especially since they run counter to what is often taught in writing classes and books. These introductions tell us almost nothing factual about the characters but make us *want to know more* about them. They rev up our theory-of-mind machinery. That simplicity is the essence of effective characterization.

The process starts with a striking first impression. Many beginner novelists insist that their hero is an everyman or everywoman, and so at first they present an ordinary character doing mundane activities or thinking routine thoughts in a commonplace way. An agent or bookstore browser scans a page or two, shrugs, puts the manuscript or book down, and moves on to the next.

Storytelling is full of paradoxes. A plot must seem true to life while in fact being much more tightly structured and definitive than real life. Dialogue must sound natural and yet avoid being as excruciatingly boring as most real-life conversation. Another paradox is that an everyman hero must be distinct and unique. How? Ishmael is an everyman narrator, a common sailor, and yet he distinguishes himself with an odd introduction and some witty commentary. Orlando is no everyman, but Gwen is something of an everywoman, yet the peanut martini is enough to light up our theory-of-mind radar.

One more: Robert Graves, in his perennial favorite *I, Claudius*, a fictionalized memoir of the Roman emperor of that name, opens the novel and introduces its protagonist with what starts out sounding like a dry recitation of biographical facts. But not for long.

I, Tiberius Claudius Drusus Nero Germanicus This-that-and-the-other (for I shall not trouble you yet with all my titles) who was once, and not so long ago either, known to my friends and relatives and associates as

> "Claudius the Idiot", or "That Claudius", or "Claudius
> the Stammerer", or "Clau-Clau-Claudius" or at best as
> "Poor Uncle Claudius"…

With that self-description and narrative voice, we know we're in for something far more interesting and fun than a straightforward historical novel about a stuffy emperor. We eagerly keep reading to see more of this character and his world.

Later, a novel usually adds new characters after the story is in play. In doing so, a common error is to stage a scene solely to introduce that character before the story yet needs him or her. Some new novelists think this is mandatory or customary, but it isn't, and such scenes often come across as tepidly utilitarian. Usually the best way to introduce characters is simply to skip the initial résumé recitation and toss them into the story at the point they become active players.

We're constantly told, "Show, don't tell." It's usually sound advice. I'd add a corollary: evoke, don't inform. If you look through your favorite novels or bestsellers from today or decades past, you will usually find they introduce their characters not with description and backstory but simply by having them enter the scene without preamble and start doing whatever the story calls for. That in itself is interesting, whereas an expository pre-intro can squelch curiosity. You'll also probably find the character performs the action not in the expected, default way but in a surprising, funny, foreboding, or otherwise arresting manner.

This is how Jonathan Franzen, in the second chapter of his bestselling novel *The Corrections*, introduces Chip, who is at the airport to pick up his pitifully aging parents.

> But to Chip Lambert, who was waiting for them just
> beyond the security checkpoint, they were killers.

Chip had crossed his arms defensively and raised one hand to pull on the wrought-iron rivet in his ear. He worried he might tear the rivet right out of his earlobe—that the maximum pain his ear's nerves could generate was less pain than he needed now to steady himself.

From there Chip slides into a sexual fantasy about a young woman who crosses his line of sight and how she might ease the torment of his parents' visit. At this point we have almost no factual information about Chip but a strong impression. We don't know if we like him—probably not—but we're certainly interested in what he's going to do and why. Instead of a generic son, Franzen has given us a distinct yet ambiguous individual who raises questions and anticipation. As well, the author has indirectly characterized the parents, not with information but with an implicit question: what did they do to make Chip think of them as killers? There's only one way to find out.

When introducing new characters and situations, it may seem handy to simply present the most likely scenario. Yet this is also the least likely way to make readers sit up and take notice or to hand our subconscious an experience worth noting, for our minds are attuned to pay attention to the different and unusual, as that's where danger and opportunity lurk. You want to surprise and intrigue readers rather than confirm their preconceptions. There's almost always habitable territory between predictable and implausible. That's where you want to operate.

Characterization

Characterization refers to how a writer puts across his characters. A common characterization error consists of reciting a load of facts about the character: a driver's-license description, a thumbnail sketch, a short (or not so short) bio. In life, following a person's first impression, which is usually based on little information, we may strike up a relationship of some sort and learn more about them, usually through watching them in action, whether at work or socially. We may hear snippets and rumors about them that may raise new questions or contradictions. Maybe we become friends and begin to swap stories, with both parties embellishing and editing to fit the listener and our motives. If we ever reach a point where we think we know all there is to know about a person, even a spouse or a lifelong friend, they become less interesting.

The science behind this is clear. For the sake of survival, any creature's attention must focus mainly on the unknowns in the environment—the stranger, the odd noise, an unexpected absence. Even after a few thousand years of so-called civilized times, our brains still function the way they evolved to do over millions of prehistoric years.

Writers often dream up a full biography of a character—their parents and siblings, marriages and divorces, and so forth. This is often a good way to get to know your own characters. But that doesn't mean this material belongs in your novel. If the story's conflicts force the past into focus, good, that's part of the story. But if not, the information risks being inert and digressive and may sap the character's mystery and mystique.

Why does Hamlet take such a roundabout approach to avenging his father's murder? There's a practical answer to that of course. If he had been straightforward about it, five minutes after his father's ghost spilled the beans, his uncle would have been bleeding to death at Hamlet's feet and the play would have been over, so that answer is no fun. These days, Hamlet often seems like a much more real, flesh-and-blood person than does his creator, whose biography is murky and whose authorship of the plays has been thrown into doubt. *Hamlet* is still popular after 400 years not because Shakespeare explained his hero's history and state of mind and the play's meaning but precisely because he did not—and so we can wonder, argue, and write postgrad theses about it. Hamlet remains a fascinating character because we'd still like to know more about him.

This is also what gives a character depth. What distinguishes a flat character from a three-dimensional or well-rounded one? Teachers have offered various answers, such as having several defining traits rather than just one, and inner conflict. True enough. But real depth comes from abiding mystery about the character: no matter how much you know, you're sure there's another deeper, hidden layer. Depth doesn't come from what you know about the character (or the real-life person) nor even from what you don't know; it comes from what *you think you don't know* about them.

The irony of Hamlet, Holden Caulfield, or any other literary character you still wonder about is that in fact there is nothing more to learn about them. The texts have been thoroughly ransacked, and the authors' opinions, if they have any, are dubious if even relevant. The depth is illusory—just as it sometimes turns out with real-life people. Depth doesn't reside in what we know about a character but in what we wonder, speculate, and hence imagine about them.

You, the author, should know your characters' backstories well and what they're all thinking and feeling in a scene so that you can decide how they will react in manner, word, and deed. You then want your readers to do the same thing—but in reverse order: to see the characters' manner and actions, and then deduce their emotions, and surmise why they might be feeling that way. Just telling readers all that short-circuits their creative participation in the story and spoils the theory-of-mind exercise.

So characterization isn't a matter of describing or explaining, since a character is often more fascinating because of what we don't know about them than what we do know. Readers can more organically get to know a character as we do people, by watching what they do, especially under stress or in crisis. These actions become clues to their personalities. Each clue builds from the previous. The clues don't always go in a straight line; people sometimes do something unexpected—yet, in hindsight, also plausible and revelatory. The new, surprising clue provides another piece to the same puzzle, and soon other pieces begin to connect with it. With a complex character, we never collect all the pieces, and the holes keep us fascinated with him, yet we always feel we're looking at the same coherent puzzle.

To come back to the evolution of the human mind, when we first meet someone, we have crucial questions to ask ourselves. Friend or foe? What does this person want from me or us? What might this person have to offer? Once the early human being thought she'd figured out the newcomer, her attention would free up to go elsewhere. In a story, however, you usually want to keep readers' attention on your characters, hence you have them remain somewhat enigmatic and unpredictable.

But not always. If you have a sleeper character, one you're saving up for a surprise unmasking, someone you don't yet want readers looking at too closely, then you might pigeonhole them quickly with a minimum of time and space—the village idiot, the mailroom drudge, the old lady who gardens all day—and readers won't give them a second look until you've set the stage.

Point of View

This subject could have waited until the later chapter on narration, but it also relates to characters and how we use them, so here goes. *Point of view* (POV) in writing refers to the character through whose eyes, ears, heart, and mind any particular scene comes to us. For example, Melville narrates *Moby-Dick* through Ishmael's POV—we see what Ishmael sees, hear his thoughts, and so on. POV is pretty straightforward if you use one character's narration for the entire novel. But a novel can also play out through the vantage of more than one character. For example, you might use the hero's POV in one chapter and the villain's in the next.

The availability of many potential POVs proves to be an irresistible temptation to many novice novelists. For example, the narration of a scene involving five characters may include relating the thoughts and inner feelings of each one of them. What's wrong with that? Yes, these days it's considered bad form, a mark of the amateur, and denigrated as head-hopping, but why? For one thing, because it can disorient readers, somewhat equivalently to jumpy camerawork or choppy editing in a movie.

Promiscuous POV brings about other, more fundamental drawbacks. One relates to the idea of stimulating reader imagination to create the inner movie. Explicitly conveying what each character in a scene thinks and feels preempts reader imagination and theory-of-mind projections. It also doesn't mimic experience, because in real life, we don't eavesdrop on the thoughts and feelings of other people, and a prime human skill is to surmise the intentions, emotions, and ideas churning inside those we have to deal with in any situation. Why deny readers the exercise, challenge, and fun? Usually because the author wants readers to absorb *his* version of the story rather than coming to their own understandings.

If it's important to suggest what a non-POV character might be thinking or feeling, the old maxim "show, don't tell" steps in. Put the clues in the character's actions, demeanor, and/or dialogue subtext. Let readers have the pleasure of proving to themselves how perceptive they are, let them stew in their uncertainty (it's called suspense), and allow them to learn from the outcome. Cultivating fertile ignorance in readers exercises theory of mind. We manage to get through our entire lives using only one POV, our own, so readers can certainly make it through a scene in a story with only one POV.

The other casualty of promiscuous POV is empathy with the main character. If readers know far more than the protagonist does, they're out of step. They're not wondering about the same questions nor uncertain about the same people. Sometimes you have a good reason to want readers to know more about something than a character or even the protagonist does, perhaps for the sake of suspense, and that's fine. But a general approach of letting readers listen in on all the characters and what they want, feel, and plan tends to make the novel wordy and slow and to lessen active reader engagement. In a novel, the fewer narrators readers have—hence the fewer characters whose inner life readers have direct access to—the more they can exercise their theory-of-mind abilities to guess what the other characters know, feel, and think.

There's also omniscient POV, or omniscience, which is written from the point of view of no particular character—perhaps the author, or God. It floats disembodied over the scene, seeing whatever, reading minds at will, floating back and forth in time. Omniscience is often used briefly to establish a novel's milieu or set a scene before it funnels down into one character's

POV. But it can also be used to narrate the story's events. Here's an excerpt from an omniscient scene in James Agee's *A Death in the Family* (1967):

> "I don't mean the whole business," [Andrew] said. "I don't know anything about that. I just mean tonight."
>
> Can't eat your cake and have it, his father thought.
>
> Like slapping a child in the face, Andrew thought; he had been rougher than he had intended.
>
> "But, Andrew dear," Mary was about to say, but she caught herself. What a thing to argue about, she thought; and what a time to be wrangling about it!
>
> Each of them realized that the others felt something of this; for a little while none of them had anything to say. Finally Andrew said, "I'm sorry."

These days omniscience is sometimes considered rather old-fashioned. And often for good reason. As novelists strive for deeper reader immersion in their stories, the distant, aloof, uninvolved, omniscient POV has become less and less useful. While it can be a more informative POV, it's often less evocative and empathic than a specific-character POV. Yet a few writers still use omniscience successfully.

A writer often decides ahead of time a story's overall POV strategy: how many POVs to use, whose, and why. Often a novel needs only one POV—the story consists of one character's ongoing experience, which readers will share. But sometimes a story literally *needs* more than one POV. The story *must* show what's happening in two different places at the same time, for example, or its intent is a broad-canvas look at the Wild

West or WWII. I emphasize *needs* because plenty of stories *can* employ multiple POV without *needing* to.

POV strategy is important. Just grabbing any handy POV for a scene is a bit like a painter dipping his brush into any old blob of paint on his palette without thinking about the overall color scheme. The more POVs you use in a novel, the more breadth you gain but the less focus you retain. Readers may partake of only a fraction of several experiences rather than a deeper immersion in one. This is the tradeoff to consider. Often the best default POV strategy is to limit the number of POVs in the story to the bare necessity, and within each scene, to use just one of those POVs.

There is also an esthetic consideration. The formal constraints of sticking with one POV per scene and using only one or a very few for the entire novel can spur writers to come up with creative ways to convey what's going on. Surely it would have been much easier for Shakespeare to have written his sonnets in free verse instead to avoid limiting himself to one formal scheme, but then would we still read them?

Predicament
and Attempted Extrication

What If?

Ersatz experience has uses beyond literature; it's a primary tool of human reasoning. We often solve problems by running scenarios through our heads of what might happen if we do this or try that. Some of Albert Einstein's most profound insights came from what he called thought experiments. In one, he imagined being inside an elevator car that was freefalling down the shaft. Then he imagined being inside the same elevator car floating free in outer space. He realized that from inside the elevator, there would be no way of distinguishing the two experiences (until the former reaches bottom). That led him to his general theory of relativity. Imagining himself chasing a light beam through space set him on the path to his special theory of relativity. Many new ventures in life and in novels are conceived with a simple what-if question.

Instinct and intuition are terms we apply to the faculty of arriving at a conclusion about something by mysterious means. Some so-called instinct or intuition is simply guesswork coupled with egotism: we take a wild stab at something, occasionally come up lucky, and call it skill. But a specific apparently intuitive skill clearly isn't just luck when it often works well. The basketball player reads the court in front of him and in a split second, without thinking about it, sees where to go, whom to pass the ball to, and when. The expert seducer knows just what to say to his or her target while the rest of us fumble for words. A good teacher visualizes the best tack to take with a new class, while the uninspired teacher plods through the lesson plan. The astute businessman can tell whom to trust and whom not to, just as the wily conman can spot a likely mark a mile away and knows which approach will work.

These skills aren't instinct, nor do we need to ascribe them to some mysterious sixth sense. They are forms of intelligence, and their conclusions are arrived at through calculation. Brain scientists often call this invisible way of thinking the *default mode*, as that's what the brain does when we're not distracting it. The default mode allows us walk down the street without crashing into other pedestrians and tripping over sidewalk hazards while our conscious minds are entirely taken up with planning what we will say and do when we get to our destination—in other words, while we conduct thought experiments to fine-tune the upcoming encounter.

The default mode process is visible to fMRI and other brain-imaging devices but seems mysterious to us only because the calculations take place out of the spotlight of consciousness, in the bustling back rooms of our nervous systems, just as a math prodigy can solve complicated arithmetic problems through means unknown to his conscious mind.

Reading a book isn't entirely a conscious, intellectual activity, and neither is writing one. Nor is it an entirely emotional, spiritual, or "artistic" (whatever that quite means) activity. Writing, like reading, should stimulate all the writer's faculties.

Just how this works differs from writer to writer. The point is to make use of all your talents, and the right ones at the right times.

The seed of a novel or other story format often arrives out of the blue. A what-if question occurs to us and begins to sprout story lines. Sometimes it's a just a fragment—a character, a peculiar relationship, a line of dialogue, a setting. Or you wake up in the middle of the night with the entire scenario vivid in your mind. (Deep brain consolidation and integration of waking experience are known functions of sleep.) This sort of brainstorm is sometimes called the *donnée*, French for something "given." And it seems supernaturally given: after being assembled and tested in the mind's secret workshop, it simply appears—*voilà!*—in the brightly lit showroom of consciousness.

But a writer doesn't have to wait for inspiration to strike. The world around us is full of what-ifs. One version of quantum theory (and an older one of metaphysical philosophy) says that anything that can happen not only will happen but already has happened, and our individual consciousnesses can't see it all because we're stuck on one tiny timeline, one *worldline*, slowly burrowing its way through this eternal, unchanging chunk of everything and always. But for us moles and our readers, there's an infinity of what-ifs waiting to be explored.

To make a good story, the what-if—the story's *premise*—must have one key attribute: that it quickly leads to a predicament, to a conflict and challenge whether physical, emotional, familial, moral, social, and/or spiritual. Your story is what happens when the character tackles the predicament, a struggle in which readers then vicariously participate. While biography or memoir is (supposedly) a factual life, fiction is an experimental life through which we can gain what adds up to a great variety of experience spawned by a what-if.

Plot

Plot isn't simply what happens, a sequential list of linked events, but how the story is structured. Most basically, a plot consists of a character's book-spanning struggle toward an objective. The Trojan War is over, and Odysseus must get back to Ithaca to save his marriage and estate. Prince Hamlet learns his uncle murdered Hamlet's father to usurp the throne and marry his mother, and he now has to set things right. A scientist who discovers a runaway asteroid headed straight for Earth must figure out how to deflect it. Not all stories need an epic plot set on a world stage, but at their core, most effective stories have this sort of structure—a character struggles for something. In a murder mystery, a detective must solve a crime; in a coming-of-age story, the hero must face a challenge, grow, and find a place for herself in the adult world.

Why plot? Because it draws on the evolutionary development of storytelling. It presents an experience of someone having to struggle to survive and how their choices turned out for them—it provides an opportunity to learn. We enjoy it because it entertains, and we learn something from it even if without noticing.

Some stories don't have a true plot. They may charm, amuse, or mesmerize us in other ways. In the 1950s, although they were not the first to do so, the French *Nouveau Roman* (new novel) movement and its cinematic counterpart the New Wave eschewed traditional plots in favor of other elements and for a while became prominent and successful.

As an artist, you should create what you want. Nor can one condemn a writer for breaking the rules, because art evolves by breaking rules—the novel itself was once a renegade art form, as were movies almost within living memory. But a storyteller, no matter how she plans to experiment, can still remain aware of a plotted story's deep-seated influence on the human mind and heart. Over the millennia and across just about every culture, a plot-like structure is how stories seem to work. If you have a good reason to depart from it, you better also have something else to take up the slack in reader engagement.

Comedy provides a good example. Some comedies are well plotted, but in others the plot is thin, nonexistent, or absurd, and the characters are caricatures, yet the laughs keep us reading, listening, or watching. I'm not talking about just a dash of wry humor here and there or a few good one-liners but out-loud laughs on every page. Likewise, erotica taps a source of engagement outside plot.

One might ask, can't the beauty of the writing alone be sufficient to engage and transport readers? For some, sure. But if you're going to write beautifully about something, why not also make that something worthwhile in its own right?

From Premise to Plot

A story's premise is the what-if seed that spawns the whole project. What if scientists were able to culture DNA from fossils and bring dinosaurs back to life? That's the premise of *Jurassic Park*. Sometimes an author gets so excited by his premise that instead of turning it into a plot, he simply takes the reader on a guided tour as the premise plays out. He might bring in a character, or a series of them, whose dialogue explains what's going on. Other writers conduct their tours through promiscuously multiple points of view, zipping readers as if on a magic carpet from one site to the next.

The magic-carpet strategy tends to lower suspense and excitement. Giving readers an intimate knowledge of the unfolding scenario lessens the amount of mystery in the novel—the very mystery that compels readers to keep reading. We may know who the villain is and what he's up to far too early in the book, and we don't learn it through the hero's thrilling detective work but simply because the author lets us listen in on the villain's plans. We ride high above the action, seeing the big picture and all sides of the conflict instead of getting personally involved in one side of the struggle. It's not much of an experience because we float above it all rather than immerse ourselves—we are rubberneckers rather than participants.

Underlying that mistake lurks a common misconception: that the premise *is* the plot. It isn't the plot—it's the seed of a plot. One turns a premise into a plot with this question: who will deal with the premise and how? For the plot isn't just the premise, it's the hero's struggle with the premise. Your premise may shimmer with brilliance, but all the more reason to give it the plot it deserves.

Starting the Plot

Some writers devise a plot but run into trouble getting it started. A common problem is excessive setup. Before shifting the plot into gear, the writer tries to set up the story in great detail. This might include exposition, backstory, settings, character sketches, and so on. Plots rarely need much setup—just as life crises rarely provide the courtesy of forewarning and preparation. In the section above on characterization, I touched on the subject of unnecessary and/or excessive preliminary information in stories. I won't repeat it here but simply add Elmore Leonard's more succinct piece of writing advice: "I just try to leave all the boring parts out."

I well understand a writer's impulse to map his territory before starting the journey, but one also has to consider the effect this has on readers. For the most part, they want the journey to start quickly because without a stake in what will happen—without taking steps down the road and seeing enough to want to continue—they have no reason to be interested in your map. The author may need to know the map in advance, but readers want to learn the territory by exploring it firsthand, through the story's events. Your job isn't to write the guidebook but to lead the expedition. Readers won't give a damn who built the subterranean temple until they're standing in the middle of it, cave lamps strapped to their heads, gazing in awe at the stalactites, wall art, pottery, and skeletons.

Because premise and plot tend to be the most engaging elements of a story, usually you want to get them underway as soon as possible. You can fill in small dollops of exposition as necessary while you move forward with the plot. If the plot's inception really does need to be delayed, you can at least hint at the underlying conflict and infuse it into the preliminaries.

A clichéd workaround that often backfires is to open the story with an exciting scene from the middle of the plot or even the climax, during which the protagonist, in a brief lull, may wonder, *How the hell did I get myself into this mess?* End of Chapter 1. Chapter 2: "Three Weeks Earlier..." and now comes all the setup. This strategy is meant to hook readers so they'll stick with the story through the setup information rather than lose interest and give up, which is what the author worried would happen if the setup were at the beginning. Why put anything boring anywhere into your story? As well, such an opening can spoil suspense by letting readers know where things are going, and it's often the most exciting scene of the novel, which can make the rest of the story disappointing.

I'll cover exposition in more detail later. My point here is to suggest you get your plot moving as soon as you can and emotionally involve readers with your story rather than delaying it with a long setup.

Plot Strength

For a thirdhand experience to hit readers as important and memorable, two elements are of key importance. The first is stakes. What do the protagonist and his people stand to gain or lose? What would be the consequences of failure? The stakes can be personal, familial, social, spiritual, and/or involve our planet's entire future. The character connection here is that readers need to care about the outcome as well. Small stakes may be enough to set your hero in motion, but will that be enough to put readers' brains on high alert? If the hero could lose her job, might that in addition trigger a domino-effect of collateral damage—her career, her neighborhood nonprofit, her apartment in which her sick grandmother also lives, and bring down the loan sharks on her ne'er-do-well brother? Think about making the stakes not just serviceable but compelling.

The second vital element is difficulty. To garner full reader cognitive participation, the protagonist's task must seem close to or even beyond impossible. If things are too easy for the protagonist, readers can shrug off the weak ordeal. I am not talking about genre or scale here. Even on a small stage with few characters, an excruciating struggle will have much deeper impact on readers or an audience than merely an inconvenient or uncomfortable situation.

First-time novelists tend to make mistakes along these lines—perfectly natural, humanitarian ones. Because they love their protagonists, they want to give them a helping hand. At the outset, even if the stakes are high, an author may make the predicament too easy to deal with. As the plot proceeds, the writer may create lucky breaks and fortuitous happenstance to ease things along. A random encounter solves a problem, a coincidence drops crucial information into the protagonist's hands. In the same vein another common error is to make the villains inept, weak, or stupid. A villain needs to be scary and daunting rather than contemptible or laughable. It's fine, perhaps even necessary, to love your characters, but your first duty is to your readers. They need your characters to go through a dire ordeal. Your job is not to ease your hero's path and pain and solve his problems for him but to push him right up to his limits and then beyond, to challenge him beyond what he thinks himself capable of. This is what will transform him, for better or for worse, and make readers' brains sit up and pay attention to your story.

Narration

A story is about significant events and memorable
moments, not about time passing.
—Daniel Kahneman, *Thinking, Fast and Slow*

A story is not an accumulation of information strung
into a narrative, but a design of events to carry us to
a meaningful climax.
—Robert McKee, *Story*

The original form of narration probably consisted of a storyteller
recounting the tales and myths of his clan to a small group of
tribespeople gathered, as in the usual rendering, around a campfire. The most modern form of narration consists of an audience
of one donning a virtual-reality headset and being dumped into
the midst of the story as it unfolds. This brings us back to the
theme of storytelling as a way to impart experience.

Written stories have a history of evolving toward a more
direct delivery of experience. In early novels, the storyteller, as
distinct from the story and its characters, would often appear
explicitly present and visible, like the campfire narrator. For
example, Cervantes opens Ch. 1 of *Don Quixote* (1605) with a
direct address to readers: "In a village of La Mancha, the name

of which I have no desire to call to mind, there lived not long since one of those gentlemen that keep a lance in the lance-rack, an old buckler, a lean hack, and a greyhound for coursing." Henry Fielding does the same sort of thing in *The History of Tom Jones* (1749), with asides like: "Reader, I think proper, before we proceed any farther together, to acquaint thee that I intend to digress..." and "I have told my reader, in the preceding chapter, that Mr Allworthy inherited a large fortune..." A less obtrusive form of authorial presence is omniscient narration (discussed earlier with point of view), which was prominent in the nineteenth and early twentieth centuries but has since dwindled.

Nowadays, most novelists refrain from appearing as themselves onstage, and thereby give readers a more direct contact with the characters and story. Yet styles of narration influence the degree of reader immersion in a story.

A *scene* is the firsthand depiction of an event, shown mainly through action and dialogue, perhaps with some interior monologue. The reader sees and hears the event as it plays out. A courtroom scene might begin something like:

> The judge banged his gavel. "Order, order in the court. Mr. Mason?"
>
> Young Perry Jr. stood up and cleared his throat. "Your Honor, esteemed members of the jury. This case..."

An event summarized in hindsight rather than conveyed as it happens isn't a scene but is usually called *narrative summary*. A summing-up like "Perry Jr. followed his strategy to the letter and argued as best he knew how, but still the jury found his client guilty" would be narrative summary—a synopsis rather than a firsthand blow-by-blow.

Many novels these days consist entirely of a series of scenes. While some attribute this change to the advent of movies and television, perhaps a more basic explanation lies in the immediacy of scenes as opposed to more remote narration. Events shown come closer to experience, and thus have greater impact, than do events told about. Yet sometimes there's still a use for narrative summary if events that don't warrant a scene need to be conveyed.

Which brings up a pitfall that dooms some first novels. The kicker to "show, don't tell" is that it's much easier for a writer to tell than to show. Telling requires only clear sentences that impart the information. Showing is rather like trying to narrate by cellphone a riot you're caught in the middle of. You've got to cover everything that happens in chronological order, convey your characters' actions, reactions, and pertinent dialogue, and imply the emotional atmosphere, all with an economy of statement that keeps up a pace befitting the scene.

Some novice writers try to find a way around this predicament without having to lapse into narrative summary. After the (unshown) event, they stage a scene in which a character, over coffee, martinis, or IV painkillers, recounts what happened at a more civilized pace. Or perhaps a character reminisces to herself about the event rather than narrating the scene as it happens. Neither ploy is as engaging for readers as a firsthand scene of the event, and this device also puts the experience at a further remove. One exception: when the scene in which the recounting occurs is itself more pivotal than the original incident, such as an interrogation, courtroom testimony, or confession.

Even in a novel consisting mostly or entirely of scenes, some novelists manage to sneak onto the stage and distract readers from the direct experience. This often manifests in little explanations. For (actual) example:

After a few steps, Murphy must have heard something,
for he stopped and peered off into the forest to the right.

As opposed to:

After a few steps, Murphy stopped and peered off into
the forest to the right.

Why not let readers intuit the reason for Murphy's action? Here's
another:

In the middle of the broadcast, the news was too much
for her to bear, and she burst into tears.

Instead, have reader empathy supply the reason:

In the middle of the news broadcast, she burst into tears.

This sort of kibitzing often pops up in dialogue:

"That's the most ridiculous thing I've ever heard in my
life," he said angrily.

Instead, a writer can show (in the scene) rather than tell (with
"angrily"):

He glared at her and leapt to his feet. "That's the most
ridiculous thing I've ever heard in my life."

The little explanatory intrusions are barely noticeable but
serve to chronically distract readers from the experience of the

story. It's like that ex-friend who used to sit next to you in the movie theater whispering commentary in your ear while you tried to watch the film.

Writer John McPhee, in the 14 Sept. 2015 issue of *The New Yorker*, put it this way:

> Ernest Hemingway's Theory of Omission seems to me to be saying to writers, "Back off. Let the reader do the creating." To cause a reader to see in her mind's eye an entire autumnal landscape, for example, a writer needs to deliver only a few words and images—such as corn shocks, pheasants, and an early frost. The creative writer leaves white space between chapters or segments of chapters. The creative reader silently articulates the unwritten thought that is present in the white space. Let the reader have the experience. Leave judgment in the eye of the beholder. When you are deciding what to leave out, begin with the author. If you see yourself prancing around between subject and reader, get lost. Give elbow room to the creative reader. In other words, to the extent that this is all about you, leave that out.

Person

I bring up this subject only because writers often ask or agonize about it. Another narration choice is *person* in its grammatical sense. First-person narration (the "I" voice, as above in "Call me Ishmael") and third-person narration (the "he" or "she" voice, as in Woolf's "He—for there could be no doubt of his sex…") are by far the most common choices, although a few novels are narrated in second person (the "you" voice, as you may have noticed in the Tom Robbins example above: "'This is the worst day of my life,' you say, as you drop a salted peanut...").

For our purposes, how does person affect reader immersion in thirdhand experience? Probably not a whole lot, since readers quickly accustom themselves to receiving the story in whatever person it happens to be written, just as we automatically accept past-tense narration as a description of the novel's present time. One might predict that second-person narration almost forces "you," the reader, into the shoes of the narrator or protagonist, but then you'd think a lot more novelists would use it. First person does seem more intimate than third, if that's an important quality for your narrator; for some novels, though, the more aloof third person may work better, especially if you want the narrator to seem mysterious or to keep his secrets from readers. Traditionally, first-person narration maintains for the entire novel, while with third person, different chapters or scenes can be narrated by different characters. But there's no so-called rule that says a novel can't have more than one first-person narrator, and it's not unusual these days.

First-person narration carries a few hidden dangers. Consider this line, originally couched in third person: "She is smart and beautiful, and although men and women constantly vie for her attention, she has few real friends, all of them fiercely protective of her privacy." When the novelist recast the novel into first person, the line became "I'm smart and beautiful, and although men and women constantly vie for my attention, I have few real friends, all of them fiercely protective of my privacy." What a different picture we now get of this person, completely unintended by the author. One small step for person, one giant leap off a cliff for the character.

The hazard doesn't apply only to what the narrator says about himself but also to how much. We all know people who, no matter how modest or self-deprecating, just plain talk about themselves too much. Instead, you can let other characters do the talking about the narrator, though not in contrived, self-serving dialogue. The narrator's reticence about himself helps create a mystique and fires up theory of mind. Meanwhile, you can direct his witty commentary and piquant insights outward, which still reveals character, but implicitly. Also, don't forget that first-person narrators, unless they're looking in a mirror, can't see their own faces, as in "My eyes shone with a strange fire as I scanned the horizon."

I suggest deciding ahead of time which person will work best for the novel you are writing. Going back later and changing person throughout an entire manuscript is a form of drudgery I, from personal experience, recommend avoiding.

Dialogue

Much has been said and written about dialogue. I will only stress some points and add a few wrinkles that relate specifically to dialogue as a way to make scenes a more vivid form of experience for readers.

Often writers have something they want said, some information or an idea, and so they have a character say it. The result is often an unconvincing scene and a compromised character. Anything a character says—or does, for that matter—should stem entirely from his or her own motives, personality, and circumstances. Turning a character into the author's mouthpiece or pawn weakens the character, reveals the wizard behind the curtain, and reminds readers that the scene is contrived rather than the real thing. Instead, find a more organic way to show what you want to get across to readers.

The main purpose of dialogue is to hint at—imply, suggest, give a glimpse of—interpersonal undercurrents among characters. After all, in real life, we rarely speak what's on our minds or hearts at the time. Instead, we're pursuing some agenda—perhaps to impress, amuse, dominate, cheer up, defuse, seduce, reject, avoid—and using conversation to push it along. When a man tells a woman that the dress she's wearing makes her look good—or chubby—he's not really commenting on fashion.

Whatever a character says, the dialogue will better serve you and the reader if it adds a new slant, a surprise, a glimpse of how the speaker's mind works, reveals a hidden element, raises a question, or at least makes us laugh. In *Apocalypse Now*, when a plane drops a line of bombs in the jungle, Robert Duval's character doesn't say, "Hey, that was some big explosion." Instead he says, "I love the smell of napalm in the morning." This dialogue gives the event, already too familiar in those days from war news footage, a jolting new angle, and it wonderfully reveals his character. Instead of asking yourself what real people *would* say in that situation, ask yourself what they *could* say that would rise above the mundane and reveal something new—and still sound perfectly natural for that character. This harks back to working within the fertile territory that lies between predictability and implausibility. Again, the brain-science reason behind it is that the unusual, even if just slightly askew, will pique reader interest and get the mind working, whereas more of the usual suggests the possibility of a nap.

Beats—little actions amid dialogue, a sidelong look, slouching in a chair—help enhance the experiential element by keeping the scene visually alive in readers' minds. A beat can add to the dialogue's subtext by hinting at unspoken undercurrents and emotions. It can also identify the speaker, thus making speaker attribution ("Bill said," etc.) unnecessary. But like most anything else, don't overdo beats to the point of distraction.

Any interchange has at least three parts. There are the spoken words, the unspoken subtext, and the mute actions—beats. You can also add a fourth element, interior monologue from the POV character. But take care to use it to show rather than to tell, and to add a new slant rather than simply to echo what has already been said or shown.

> His hands lingered on her shoulders as he helped her on with her coat. "We're going to have a great time tonight."
>
> She took his arm and smiled. Handsome, and charming too—this would be a fun date.

In the I.M. above, all we get is a pointless echo of her actions. Or:

> His hands lingered on her shoulders as he helped her on with her coat. "We're going to have a great time tonight."
>
> She took his arm and smiled. Handsome, in a creepy way.

If you rely too heavily on spoken words and interior monologue, you tend to tell too much and thereby preempt any need to read between the lines, which in turn stifles reader imagination and audience participation. Silence and unspoken implication can be far more powerful.

> To say, "Leave the room," is less expressive than to point to the door. Placing a finger on the lips is more forcible than whispering, "Do not speak." A beck of

the hand is better than, "Come here." No phrase can convey the idea of surprise so vividly as opening the eyes and raising the eyebrows. A shrug of the shoulders would lose much by translation into words.
~ Herbert Spencer, *Philosophy of Style*

As for the words, phrasing, and manner a character uses in dialogue, the days of dramatic declamation are long gone—unless, of course, your character happens to be a dramatic declaimer. For a scene to work as experience, the character must talk like that character would talk in that situation. This doesn't mean you should use phonetic spelling to imitate accent, which tends to be distractive and condescending. Once you have worked the dialogue's gist to fit the character's motives, personality, and present situation, the most important variables are word choices and phrasing. Keep in mind that we don't talk the way we write, with well-formed sentences in premeditatedly logical sequence. The spoken words in dialogue have no obligation to be grammatical, sensible, or pertinent to the previously spoken line. They only have to sound like that character's words in those circumstances.

But let's not take that too far. Novelists and scriptwriters have to deal with an infernal paradox: life is 90 percent boring; a novel, play, or movie has to *appear* lifelike but also has to be 100 percent nonboring. Later, I will go further into reality vs. art, but it especially concerns dialogue, since in real life, other people's conversations have consistently won the award for most boring thing in the universe—far more boring than silence. The way around this in dialogue, though, is simple. Just don't write the boring stuff. How are you, how're the kids, nice day, might rain, sciatica acting up—just skip it. That is, unless you have a good reason for it, such as a character's deliberately avoiding the crucial topic, at which point the chitchat is no longer boring but suspenseful. Readers won't notice the absence of small talk, they'll just think you write snappy dialogue.

Likewise, in real life, we make inane, mundane, or obvious remarks and utter inert words and phrases to keep the conversational carrier wave humming, defuse tension, and avoid uncomfortable silences. However, while in life we want conversation to be comfortable, in a novel or script we want to highlight the tension and undercurrents that the polite noises muffle. So be very, very sparing with mundane chitchat in written dialogue. Silence often works much better. Again, readers won't miss or even notice the omitted padding, they'll be too engrossed in the drama.

Dialogue doesn't consist of writing true-to-life conversation but is the art of writing scintillating conversation that *seems* true to life and so heightens the experience but avoids the banality, repetition, and inert sounds of most real-life conversation.

Even if you write terrific dialogue, you can still mar it by trying to tart it up with writerly accoutrements. Chief among these is unnecessary or verbose speaker attribution ("Granny said," etc.). In dialogue, readers need to know who is speaking, and promptly enough not to become confused. However, writers are not obligated to provide speaker attribution when it's not needed. If context, a beat, or the 1-2-1-2 pattern of two-person conversation instantly identifies the speaker, attribution is redundant. The same goes for trippingly clever variations on *said* and accompanying adverbs, he intoned ominously. Except occasionally for comedic purposes, you want readers absorbed in the interplay among the characters rather than scrutinizing your literary acrobatics—you want them experiencing the story rather than experiencing the nuts and bolts of your writing.

Exposition

Writers sometimes assume there are two parts to storytelling: the story itself, and then all the other stuff we're supposed to do, such as setting, backstory, thumbnail character sketches, exposition, and description. But there is no such dichotomy either explicit or implicit. Exposition isn't a formal requirement, there for its own sake. We don't need to halt the story to convey characterization and backstory. Too many first-timers put the narrative on hold and go off into pages of background information on characters and setting. Yet as bestselling British author Ian McEwan says, "Narrative tension is primarily about withholding information." Which runs smack into the chronic bugbear of many writers, both beginners and veterans—exposition. To tell or not to tell, how much, and when?

A novelist's task in writing a story isn't so much to give readers a guided tour, packed with running commentary, as it is to immerse them in an alternate life and let them live it, feel it, and learn from it as best they can. More than knowledge, you're giving them experience from which to synthesize their own very personal understanding. Real-life experience is often made more vivid because of a lack of information. Who are these people? What do they want? Why are they staring at me?

Even before starting to write, storytellers often have thought up a lot of backstory for their tale. The setting may be one they know well from experience or have thoroughly researched. And of course there's all the character information I talked about earlier. Writers are often eager to explain all these things to readers. Too little too late may be a sin in public relations, but too much too soon is what sends exposition to hell.

Obvious when you think about it but easily overlooked, the process of writing a novel is entirely different from reading one. Often an author works out ahead of time all the background and backstory, knows the biographies of even minor characters, has the keys to all the skeleton closets, and plans the eventual outcome. You may have to figure all this out in advance if you want to create multidimensional characters and elegantly woven plot lines. Once you've done all that preliminary groundwork, your natural communicative impulse is put it all down on paper for your readers so that you and they are on the same page. Except you're not on the same page. They're starting to read the first page, and you've finished writing the last page.

It's a natural but misguided impulse to let your readers know as much as possible about your novel's main characters and setting as soon as you can. The thankless irony of this situation is that most readers neither need nor want the information—at least not so much nor so soon. Readers are like children—they want the good stuff, they want it now, and they don't care what you think is best for them. The good stuff is story—dramatic character interaction and intriguing situations.

But don't readers have to know all the background to get into the story? In a word, no. In fact, it's the other way around. You have to get them into the story before they'll be interested in the exposition. It's the difference between sitting in an auto dealership listening to a salesman drone on about a car's features, or trying out all those features while taking a test drive. Let's get this story on the road.

The point of a story isn't to inform readers of events and ideas, but to immerse them in what is as close as possible to an actual, meaningful experience—which in real life often has far more questions than answers. Narration then usually works best not as informative discourse but as a depiction of action, speech, and perhaps a character's thoughts while they occur rather than

Peter Gelfan

as the author's explanation of the event. Eliminate the middleman and put readers right into the scene with the characters.

Your test subjects, your guinea pigs, your beta readers, may comment along the lines of, "In the opening chapter, I really wished I knew more about Sarah Jane," and so you decide you better add some exposition. Suppose a horror writer got a beta critique, "Stephen, this story gave me nightmares for a week, you better tone it down," would he? If you create a compelling character, of course your beta readers wish they knew more about her, and that's why they kept reading. You want to preserve and play on their wanting to know rather than relieve their curiosity as fast as you can.

Keep in mind that fiction doesn't work the same way as nonfiction. Nonfiction says what it means. Fiction is a less direct and more embracive method of communication. It appeals to all reader faculties—emotions, intellect, imagination, senses, intuition, and so forth—and instead of spoon-feeding its message, it attempts to elicit the desired effects from the readers themselves. The basic technique is to create characters and a story that pull readers in, and from their vicarious experiences with the characters, they learn something. Explicitly telling them what they should learn short-circuits the process.

This principle often translates into that oldest of maxims for writers—show, don't tell. I once did an informal poll asking people how much of *Moby-Dick* they had read. Most had gotten partway through. Where did they stop? The majority cited the expository chapter on cetology, which paused the story to relate the natural history of whales.

Unlike nonfiction, storytelling doesn't run on information, but on its opposite: mystery. I'm not talking about mystery as a genre, but as the essential quality in all fiction that cultivates curiosity, stimulates the imagination, invites participation, builds

58

suspense, makes us avid to find out what's going to happen, and generally keeps readers reading. The urge to inform readers runs up against the fact that any novel needs plenty of mystery, suspense, and surprise. Readers need to wonder and care about what is going to happen, or what has already happened that they don't yet know about but hope to. Surprise of course depends on prior mystery and suspense, whose essential mechanics are so crude that they're often overcomplicated. Suspense and mystery are just fancy words for ignorance. The math is simple: the more information you give readers, the less ignorant they will be, hence the less mystery and suspense your novel will have. According to W.H. Auden, "Knowledge may have its purposes, but guessing is always more fun than knowing."

Ignorance is humankind's biggest barrier to survival and success. Where's the prey? Is that other tribe going to attack, and when? With that storm approaching, should we head for the forest, where we might find food, or for the mountain, where we can shelter in a cave? Or: What was that look my boss gave me today? What does my daughter do with that rowdy crowd she hangs out with? What's the best way to get an agent to read my manuscript? If stories provide a risk-free form of play that exercises the human specialty of projecting actions and consequences into the future to solve problems related to survival, then every step of the journey should be fraught with questions, not only about how the story turns out, but also about character, motive, backstory, and—perhaps most importantly—what readers would do in the hero's or villain's shoes.

Because ignorance is the enemy and knowledge is the best defense, it is a common human trait to show off how much we know. Appearing knowledgeable adds to one's perceived value as an ally, friend, or potential mate, hence raises our status. This may subconsciously spur writers to explain what could more evocatively be left to readers to figure out or imagine. A story, like life, is driven more by questions than by answers. People, whether real or fictional, fascinate us not because we know all about them but because we'd like to, and situations engage our intellects and tear at our hearts because of their uncertainties.

A simple rule of thumb for exposition, similar to the need-to-know principle from spy stories: tell readers nothing unless you must, not until you have to, and only in the smallest possible quantity. Are there exceptions? Of course, but they should stem from the needs of story itself and not from the writer's itch to blab.

Then, instead of dry exposition, make the revelation as dramatic and exciting as possible. The information that comes out in a novel can be likened to the candy in a piñata. The real joy isn't in the candy itself but in all the fun to be had in getting it out. Simply informing readers of what's what and why is like handing kids the candy without letting them run around blindfolded, screaming like maniacs, flailing clubs at some poor paper burro. It spoils the party.

Often the most practical attitude toward exposition is simply to push ahead with the story. When you come to a place in the narrative where backstory or other information is *needed* because the immediate storyline *requires* it *now*, then bring it out in an exciting way—an interrogation, blackmail, a confession—which then makes it part of the thrills rather than a forced break from them.

Realism

Man is eminently a storyteller. His search for a purpose, a cause, an ideal, a mission and the like is largely a search for a plot and a pattern in the development of his life story—a story that is basically without meaning or pattern. ~ Eric Hoffer, *The Passionate State of Mind*

What do we mean by "reality"? The glib answer: that which conforms to the actual world around us. But we're not in direct touch with the hypothetical actual world around us. Our sense organs receive stimuli presumably from something out there and relay them to the brain. The brain then constructs a full-sensory simplification of the information and presents to our awareness a virtual reality that we are capable of manipulating well enough to survive for a while. As an analogy, air traffic controllers coordinate the movements of thousands of planes a day by watching and manipulating a virtual simplification consisting of glowing dots moving around on a two-dimensional screen.

So is there such a thing as reality? That's a perennial philosophical conundrum, but for our purposes here, it doesn't matter. Reality is what readers will accept as real enough for a story—and what the nonconscious parts of their minds will accept as an experience worth remembering.

We first looked at realism in the section above on dialogue, which has to seem realistic yet avoid the humdrum, mundanity, and repetitiousness of real life. The same thing goes for your entire story. Real life is also pretty boring most of the time, but unlike a novel, it can't be closed and laid on the table when we've had enough of it for now. No art form is truly true to life, and if all we needed was true life, we wouldn't have a reason to read, nor we would we be humans and able to learn hard life-and-death lessons from ersatz or imagined experience.

Readers understand that a story is a contrivance, but you want them to forget that while they read, listen, or watch.

Your audience primarily wants to be entertained by a good story—and I mean entertainment in the broadest sense, not just pleasant diversion. We can call it esthetic appreciation, but I think that tends to both obscure and dandify what we're talking about: giving the reader pleasure, pain, and insight of various kinds. A story must consistently stimulate a range of faculties—emotion, imagination, esthetics, the senses, intellect, sense of humor, memory, even the spiritual. You want to give readers as much intense involvement as you can at all times. Every chapter, every scene, every conversation, every action, every thought, every sentence, and every word should be designed to do that. Never have a character do or say anything simply because in real life they would have—because most of real life isn't at all entertaining, insightful, enlightening, or even interesting. The characters, action, and dialogue must *seem* natural and realistic but must invisibly depart from realism by always being worthwhile.

Realism—the illusion of reality—doesn't have a lot to do with genre. Science fiction and fantasy can seem realistic if the characters are believable, readers can empathize with them, and their creator stays true to the rules of his fictive world. Gratuitous authorial bells and whistles, such as messing with chronology and directly addressing readers, reminds them all too vividly of the contrivance. So do inconsistencies, anomalies, awkward writing, and grammatical errors.

One of the great pleasures of reading is to later look back and be able to understand the story's events in a whole new light. This process also helps the mind digest, correlate, and remember the story's implicit lessons. As you write, keep in mind how readers will reinterpret what happened and why, so that everything falls into place without any anomalies. The trick is to make both versions perfectly plausible as the story plays out, and yet keep readers from seeing the true version until your climactic revelation.

A story is distilled experience. Boil away all of reality's mundane, humdrum, routine, and boring parts (as we have all at times wished we could do) to leave only the exciting and meaningful, and there's the essence of story.

Voice

Beyond the story itself lies another layer of storytelling and experience, the fraught and highly subjective topic of a writer's voice. Agents, publishers, and reviewers are always looking for a strong new voice to champion. But what is it?

Narrative voice can be summed up as the impression the writing gives of the storyteller—confident or hesitant, wry or earnest, angry or witty, aloof or scrappy, wise or naïve, and so forth. It often adds up to how the writer seems to feel about the characters and events, which is important to the story because readers will often adopt those feelings or perhaps bridle against them. Writing voice is somewhat equivalent to stage or screen presence. Think of a time you heard raconteur tell a story. You listen to the story, but at the same time, you infer a lot about the storyteller. If he seems funny, clever, or full of surprises, you may be more likely to stay around and listen than if he comes across as nervous, pompous, petty, nasty, or self-serving. Voice largely determines the regard the listener or reader will have for the storyteller and thus to some degree for the story. Of course, not everyone will come up with the same opinion. One person's guru can be another's charlatan. But generally, successful writers are admired for a strong, distinct voice, one that won't let you easily walk away from the story or soon forget it.

Some beginner writers think that to have a strong voice, they have to interject themselves into the narration with asides to readers, flashy ornamentations to the prose, arcane vocabulary, or other distractions. This rarely if ever enhances readers' experiences with the story itself.

A compelling, unique voice on its own can be a reason to venture into a book, while a weak one can soon turn readers away. Although a novelist isn't usually as noticeable as an in-person storyteller, it's the same idea: the storyteller herself as an asset or liability to the whole package. In first-person narration, the voice of the author and the narrator can be hard to pry apart, and there's no need to do so, although it can be fun and instructive to try. In a third-person novel, they are often quite distinct. For example, the hero might be a sunny optimist while the authorial voice seems cynical, as with Candide and Voltaire.

In humankind's evolution as adroit, prolific storytellers and story-listeners who benefit from thirdhand experience, where might voice fit in? It comes back to theory of mind. In cave days, or today at work or at social gatherings, while we listen to and parse a story, another part of our minds is scoping out the storyteller. Who is this guy? Why is he telling this story? Is he believable? What does he have to gain by making us believe the story? Your verdict on the storyteller will to a large degree determine the validity and relevance you grant the story. A strong voice might evoke the author as a leader or a wise person, while a weak one, a bookish scribbler.

Children seem to be born credulous, since it's probably safer for them to heed without question what their parents tell them—hence fairy tales, fables, and scary lies to elicit obedience. But as we grow older, we become more knowledgeable and more capable of evaluating the reliability of what we hear from others. Writers get a slight break since the conviction that "it must be true, I read it in a book" usually lingers on a bit longer than the illusion of parental infallibility.

Fiction is explicitly an invented tale, so how does voice apply to credibility? Someone once said that novelists tell the truth by lying. They illuminate truth with a made-up story. Some stories aren't meant to be believed—say, a ridiculous comedy, an outrageously exaggerated adventure, or a silly but fun fantasy, all intended as light entertainment. But for most fiction whose writers hope to have a deeper impact on readers or viewers—and this can certainly include genre fiction as well as so-called literary fiction—theory-of-mind calculations will be in play for readers, not only in regard to the characters but also the storyteller.

As we take in someone's story on its own merits, another dynamic is in play: how much credence do we grant the story-teller, hence the story? Is this just entertaining nonsense or so distant from my concerns that it doesn't matter if it's true or not? Or does the storyteller seem believable and earnest, and her story could one day pertain to my wellbeing? There's also an emotional response: do we like this narrator, do we want to listen to her story, do we want to believe her—and do we want to hear her next story? This overall evaluation, even if not consciously calculated, will largely determine the depth and duration of a story's impact on its audience.

The most common buzzword for voice in fiction is prob-ably "authentic." An authentic voice convincingly implies that the writer knows what he's talking about and is person-ally familiar with people like his characters, places like his set-tings, and situations similar to his plot. The world of his novel is or has been his world, and he has probably been through its wringer and come out alive. To borrow another term from spy fiction, the author comes across as a reliable source.

Fiction readers are demanding creatures. They want their made-up stories to be as close to truth as possible—sort of like vegetarian meat. If they have to pick between two gritty detective novels, one by an ex-cop and the other by an MFA who has always lived in the nice part of town, you know which book most of them will carry to the cashier. Book-jacket bios try to bolster author mystique. For nonfiction, all that's needed may be a list of academic degrees, high positions, and awards—the experts agree, this writer knows her stuff. For fiction, other than previous books published, credentials get more elusive. Some bios include a long list of jobs the author has had: lumberjack in Siberia, goat wrangler in Mongolia, fry cook on Air Force One, poet-in-residence at MI-6's spy academy, yoga instructor to the Vatican, and so on. This guy has seen it all and done it all, and I better pay attention so that some of it might rub off on me. Other bios give almost no information, perhaps suggesting an intriguing secret life.

But the main way readers judge the authenticity of an author, and therefore of a novel, is by his or her writing voice. Ernest Hemingway serves as a good example. He's generally regarded as "the real thing," a man's man who went to war, hunted big game, hung out in between-the-wars Paris with literary legends, had big tragic love affairs, went fishing with Fidel Castro, and exited this world on his own terms. But his voice doesn't depend on his bio. It permeates his writing.

How does a writer forge an authentic voice? It's a daunting subject. Some successful authors give encouragement along the lines of, "After you've published your third or fourth novel, you begin to find your voice"—a big help for someone trying to get their first novel into print. "Write what you know" is a well-worn piece of advice but certainly limiting and probably lazy. Googling "narrative voice" is like searching a flea market for a true gem.

We have all read novels that for the sake of authenticity give detailed descriptions of towns, buildings, cars, or equipment.

> Jake Snade tucked the Smith & Wesson 460XVR into his attaché case. The pistol weighed 82.5 ounces unloaded, and sporting a 10.5-inch barrel with an adjustable rear sight, it boasted the highest muzzle velocity of any production revolver on earth at 2330 feet per second. For what he had in mind, he would only need one or two of the five .460 magnum rounds impatiently waiting in the cylinder.

So, the writer spent a few minutes on Google, and it sounds better than "Jake grabbed his really big gun and stuck it in his briefcase," but does it add up to an authentic voice? Contrast it with a passage from *For Whom the Bell Tolls*:

> He reached over for the submachine gun, took the clip out that was in the magazine, felt in his pocket for clips, opened the action and looked through the barrel, put the clip back into the groove of the magazine until it clicked, and then looked down the hill slope. Maybe half an hour, he thought. Now take it easy.
>
> Then he looked at the hillside and he looked at the pines and he tried not to think at all.

For me, that "click" brings the description of the gun into the realm of authentic experience. Even more convincing are Robert Jordan's implicit thoughts and feelings about what he's about to do with the gun. Hemingway doesn't fondle the equipment. He's more concerned with his characters. War isn't a spectacle but human tragedy.

As an aside, the main experience offered by some novels, it seems to me, is voice itself. Such novels may or may not have something akin to a plot, but the most vivid experience they give readers is what it must be like to be the author/protagonist, what the world looks like through their eyes. Some of Henry Miller's novels hit me this way, and William Burroughs's *Naked Lunch*, and I don't know how else to relate to James Joyce's *Finnegan's Wake.*

Articles and books by academics and critics will often focus on the author as much as on his or her work. These analyses often delve into not only the author's writing and voice but also history, biographies, memoirs, collected correspondence, and even interviews. Such psychoanalysis can be very interesting and amounts to a scholarly approach to theory of mind. For a student, it can deepen understanding and appreciation. But for a writer in the here and now struggling to be published or widely read, it's just a pleasant fantasy, and meanwhile your work has to speak for itself.

It's difficult to talk about how to improve one's writing voice, because the harder you try to class it up, the more likely you are to sound phony. If readers can see your efforts to appear authentic, literary, witty, or profound by using gratuitously arcane vocabulary, convoluted or stilted syntax, strained figures of speech, or knockoffs from other writers, then clearly you have not yet attained those qualities, or worse, are a poseur. Even if you're pretty damn good, being a showoff is a confession of insecurity. Improving voice takes a more Zen approach, trying by not trying, or at least not trying too hard.

Other books offer specific advice on improving voice. My main message on this topic is that voice matters. You can think of it as similar to characterization, as readers apply their theory-of-mind abilities to the author rather than to a character.

Since many of the bad habits I covered earlier in this piece betray a lack of self-confidence, weeding them out of your writing is one good way to improve voice without directly monkeying with it. This applies even to little errors in grammar and typos. An author's appearing at all incompetent, amateurish, or slapdash will undermine voice and the story's apparent validity. "The real reason for good usage in writing is that if you do not achieve it, your educated reader will be thinking of you, not of the point you're trying to make." ~ John W. Velz, Shakespeare scholar.

A good start to improving voice is to say something worthwhile in a fresh way. Then, when rereading your own writing, for every sentence, ask yourself, "Can I say this any better?"

Coda

There's far more to good writing and storytelling than just brain science. But without it, we've to some extent been flying blind. The intention of this treatise is neither to rewrite the so-called rules nor to bolster the old ones, but to bring about a clearer view of reading and writing for writers to use in developing their own methods. There are many ways to write a story that will create vivid experiences for readers, and a broad palette of different styles with which to give it a unique flavor. But it helps to know what you are trying to do.

You may rebut some of the points I've made, perhaps by citing successful writers who do just the opposite. Any "rule" about writing or any art should be prefaced with "maybe," "sometimes," or, at most, "usually." The point isn't what you should do, but what works most effectively for what you want to accomplish with readers. On the other hand, over the centuries, a lot of good, smart writers have come up with and relied on some general principles, and so we should be careful not to assume that a desire to flout one of those principles is sufficient reason to do so. You should certainly play devil's advocate in regard to whatever I or anyone else tells you about writing or any other subject. All writers get away with something. But not-yet-successful writers might lean toward trying to get away with as little as possible, because you probably won't.

Does that mean you should attempt to write conventionally? No, because that's a sure way to sound hackneyed. But you might think about what I'm saying and see if it could apply to your writing. Then pick your battles strategically. Decide what's most important to you in what you're writing, how the so-called rules might help you, and where you must—*must*—break the general principles of effective storytelling to accomplish your aims.

Some writers decide to do things differently. They risk defying convention, perhaps for the sake of novelty or experiment or because their vision for the story seems to need a radical approach. Some readers seek the new, while others want variety only in characters, plots, and settings without upsetting the usual architecture. Many book reviewers appreciate getting something new and different, as it's a change from the usual and opens new avenues for analysis and criticism. But if they find it doesn't work for them, they'll most likely say so.

A recent example of innovation was the rise (or reappearance), in the latter half of the twentieth century, of metafiction, which plays on the implicit conventions of the novel, such as the distinction between the novel's world and our "real" world. Sometimes innovation will spark interest and debate and generate a buzz, or it will meet with immediate dismissal. Rarely, it will incrementally change the future of literature. Novelty itself might boost your novel or shoot it down from the start. So, faced with the predictable unpredictability of the literary world, what should you do? Perhaps the most straightforward and honest (if that has anything to do with it) strategy is to write your story in what seems to you to be the most effective possible way to bring about the desired response in readers.

However you approach your storytelling, it's helpful to keep in mind that you're creating experiences for readers. It rarely works well to just plod along transcribing a scene, describing a person, explaining an idea, or working your own agenda without dovetailing it with readers' desires. With every scene, every conversation, every line, deliver something of value to readers, create a desired effect, whether excitement, peace, disgust, horror, fear, laughter, titillation, euphoria, grief, insight, epiphany, and/or inspiration. They will enjoy every page, and whether they know it or not, they will likely come away wiser.

> Human murder is different from that practiced by other animals. We are the only species in which the intended victim can concoct a story to save himself.
>
> —Brain scientist Leonard Mlodinow, *Elastic*

Further Reading

This list is a selection of nontechnical books with portions directly related to science and storytelling. There are of course many more scientific books, articles, and papers regarding human brains, cognition, communication, and the evolution of our culture, all of which have a bearing on writing.

Brian Boyd, *On the Origin of Stories*
Jonathan Gottschall *The Storytelling Animal*
Daniel Kahneman, *Thinking, Fast and Slow*
Leonard Mlodinow, *Elastic*
Steven Pinker *The Sense of Style*
Robert M. Sapolsky, *Behave*
Robert Trivers, *The Folly of Fools*
Lisa Cron, *Wired for Story*
Antonio Damasio, *The Strange Order of Things*
Michael S. Gazzaniga, *The Consciousness Instinct*
Nate Silver, *The Signal and the Noise*
Leonard Mlodinow, *Subliminal*
Nicholas Epley, *Mindwise*

Acknowledgements

Renni Browne, who got me started as an editor at The Editorial Department. Ross Browne, who kept me awash in manuscripts. My clients, who trusted me to edit their work with care. Thank you.

About the Author

Peter Gelfan has been a book editor for more than 25 years, editing for writers ranging from bestselling authors to first-timers. His novel *Found Objects* was published in 2013 and *Monkey Temple* in 2019. He lives in New York City, where he continues to write, work as a freelance book editor, and tutor writing in a public high school as part of PEN's Writers in the Schools program.

CPSIA information can be obtained
at www.ICGtesting.com
Printed in the USA
LVHW031535261021
701602LV00008B/1650

9 781955 196673